Thomas Kinsella

Readings in Poetry

Peppercanister 25

Peppercanister Books

Distributed in Ireland by
The Dedalus Press,
13 Moyclare Rd., Baldoyle, Dublin 13

in the United Kingdom by
Carcanet Press Limited,
28-34 Cross St., Manchester M2 7AQ

in the United States and Canada by
Dufour Editions Inc.,
P.O. Box 7, Chester Springs, Pennsylvania 19425

First published 2006

The Dedalus Press
ISBN 1 904556 47 7

Carcanet Press Ltd.
ISBN 1 85754 865 5

Printed in Ireland by Johnswood Press Ltd., Dublin

The Dedalus Press receives financial support from
The Arts Council, An Chomhairle Ealaíon, Dublin

Note

It was proposed to accompany the reading of ‘Prufrock’ with the text of the poem, the lines numbered as with the other poems – as a convenience to the reader, the poem being widely available. Permission for this was refused by the publisher. It is suggested that the reader should take the trouble of making a numbered copy, so as to follow the reading closely

. . .of all trades, literature at present demands the least talent or information; and, of all modes of literature, the manufacturing of poems. The difference indeed between these and the works of genius is not less than between an egg and an egg-shell; yet at a distance they both look alike.

Now it is no less remarkable than true, with how little examination works of polite literature are commonly perused, not only by the mass of readers, but by men of first rate ability, till some accident or discussion[1] have roused their attention, and put them on their guard. And hence individuals below mediocrity not less in natural power than in acquired knowledge; nay, bunglers who have failed in the lowest mechanic crafts, and whose presumption is in due proportion to their want of sense and sensibility; men, who being first scribblers from idleness and ignorance, next become libellers from envy and malevolence, have been able to drive a successful trade in the employment of the booksellers. . .

from **Biographia Literaria**, Chapter II
Samuel Taylor Coleridge

---

[1] In the course of one of my Lectures, I had occasion to point out the almost faultless position and choice of words, in Pope's original compositions, particularly in his *Satires* and *Moral Essays*, for the purpose of comparing them with his translations of Homer, which, I do not stand alone in regarding as the main source of our *pseudo*-poetic diction. . . Among other passages, I analysed sentence by sentence, and almost word by word, the popular lines,

As when the moon, refulgent lamp of night, etc.

(*Iliad* viii)

. . . The impression on the audience in general was sudden and evident; and a number of enlightened and highly educated persons, who at different times afterwards addressed me on the subject, expressed their wonder, that truth so obvious should not have struck them before. . . so much had they been accustomed, in reading poetry, to receive pleasure from the separate images and phrases successively, without asking themselves whether the collective meaning was sense or nonsense. . .

Preface

The Norton Anthology of English Literature (New York, London, 2000), introducing the selection of William Morris's work, describes 'The Defense of Guenevere' as "a remarkable book of poetry. . . which some critics regard as the finest book of Pre-Raphaelite verse". And William Morris has an established reputation, with a place in literary history.

Selecting at random from 'The Defense of Guenevere':

…Her voice was low at first, being full of tears,
But as it cleared, it grew full loud and shrill,
Growing a windy shriek in all men's ears,

A ringing in their startled brains, until
She said that Gauwaine lied, then her voice sunk,
And her great eyes began again to fill,

Though still she stood right up, and never shrunk,
But spoke on bravely, glorious lady fair!
Whatever tears her full lips may have drunk,

She stood, and seemed to think, and wrung her hair,
Spoke out at last with no more trace of shame,
With passionate twisting of her body there:

"It chanced upon a day that Launcelot came
To dwell at Arthur's court: at Christmas time
This happened; when the heralds sung his name,

"'Son of King Ban of Benwick,' seemed to chime
Along with all the bells that rang that day,
O'er the white roofs, with little change of rhyme.

"Christmas and whitened winter passed away,
And over me the April sunshine came,
Made very awful with black hail-clouds, yea.

"And in Summer I grew white with flame,
And bowed my head down – Autumn, and the sick
Sure knowledge things would never be the same,

"However often Spring might be most thick
Of blossoms and buds, smote on me, and I grew
Careless of most things, let the clock tick, tick. . .

Paying close attention to the narrative : there is a verbal excess in the first four lines, growing to an extreme in line 52, and pausing on the rhyme 'until' in expectation of a revelation or climax; all acceptable pending a revelation of the cause. This dissipates in slackness, in the flat statement 'that Gauwaine lied'; the anticlimax followed by a succession of unlikely images, rhyming bluntly on 'sunk'; the heroine's figure standing 'right up'; an assurance that she 'never shrunk'; her full lips possibly having drunk the full contents of her great eyes; and – as she 'seems' to think, while wringing her hair and twisting her body passionately – uttering a statement made increasingly awkward by the demands of rhyme and metre: where the singing of heralds seems to chime, church bells rhyme, April is made very awful with black hail-clouds and an unlikely expletive, while in Summer the heroine grows white with flame, and Spring is thick with blossoms; the demands of rhyme increasing to the grotesque in lines 71, 73 and 75.

It would seem impossible to accept this as serious verse. Likewise with 'The Haystack in the Floods', the other poem in the anthology's selection from Morris's work. And possible to accept a reputation on the basis of such poetry only on condition that the poems are not read closely.

*

In the useful five-volume anthology *Poets of the English Language* edited by W.H.Auden and Normal Holmes Pearson (Eyre and Spottiswoode, London, 1952) the introduction lists Henry David Thoreau among ". . . the first important American poets. . ."

Of the eighteen poems in the anthology's selection from Thoreau the following are three:

Among the worst of men that ever lived

Among the worst of men that ever lived,
However we did seriously attend,
A little space we let our thoughts ascend,
Experienced our religion and confessed
'Twas good for us to be there – be anywhere:
Then to a heap of apples we addressed
And cleared the topmost rider *sine* care,
But our Icarian thoughts returned to ground
And we went on to heaven the long way round.

Tall Ambrosia

Among the signs of autumn I perceive
The Roman wormwood (called by learned men
Ambrosia elatior, food for gods, –
For to impartial science the humblest weed
Is as immortal once as the proudest flower –)
Sprinkles its yellow dust over my shoes
As I cross the now neglected garden.
– We trample under foot the food of gods
And spill their nectar in each drop of dew –
My honest shoes, fast friends that never stray
Far from my couch, thus powdered, countryfied,
Bearing many a mile the marks of their adventure,
At the post-house disgrace the Gallic gloss
Of those well dressed ones who no morning dew
Nor Roman wormwood ever have been through,
Who never walk but are *transported* rather –
For what old crime of theirs I do not gather.

Great Friend

I walk in nature still alone
    And know no one,
Discern no lineament nor feature
    Of any creature.

Though all the firmament
    Is o'er me bent,
Yet still I miss the grace
    Of an intelligent and kindred face.

I still must seek the friend
Who does with nature blend,
Who is the person in her mask,
He is the man I ask.

Who is the expression of her meaning,
Who is the uprightness of her leaning,
Who is the grown child of her weaning.

The center of this world,
The face of nature,
The site of human life,
Some sure foundation
And nucleus of a nation –
At least a private station.

We twain would walk together
Through every weather,
And see this aged nature
Go with a bending stature.

Again, it would seem impossible to accept these as serious poems. Vapid, virtually automatic utterances from a commonplace sensibility, characterised by an intellectual, sensual, imaginative and technical disorder, they disintegrate under the slightest of rational demands.

As, in 'Great Friend': in attempting to follow the thread of imagery from the third stanza, where nature, vague and feminine, is masking or concealing (or concealing the lack of) a male friend, how – in the fourth 'stanza' – is the reader to take the 'uprightness of her leaning' or 'the grown child of her weaning'? Except as victims of the felt need to rhyme with 'meaning'. There is a disorder or emptiness in the perception, culminating in the formal capitulation and poetic chaos of the final three stanzas, or units. A chaos and disorder not by reference to any standard or external requirements, but by reference to the order that the poem itself is trying to establish.

The survival as 'important' of a reputation based on such poems would seem possible only as a received opinion: again, as with the poems of William Morris, only on condition that the poems are not read closely.

*

W.H.Auden, in *The Dyer's Hand*, has said that it is unnecessary to attack bad art, 'because it will perish anyway. . . Some books are undeservedly forgotten; none are undeservedly remembered.' But false reputations are established, and can survive through inertia. And there would be pressure, even now, against the blunt judgement that William Morris was a bad poet, and Thoreau not really a poet at all; that such poetic reputations as they have are undeserved. Ideally one would merely point at the poems. But it is easier to accept established opinion than to meet the requirements of art, reading and assessing individual poems closely; easier to make general connections and discuss issues than to take note – at each encounter with the text – of the accumulation of particulars and the relation of detail to structure. So that it is not enough to point at the poems.

*

The following close readings of a few notable works are responses of the kind suggested by Coleridge for the appreciation of a poem. They are 'primary' readings – a reenactment in each case of a response to the poem, taking account of the textual detail of content, method and structure, the data noted as they are given and accumulate. The text of the poem is taken as initiating an act of communication, and the reading is offered as a completion of the act, the poem read at its own pace. There are no generalisations; no considerations with *The Love Song of J. Alfred Prufrock*, for example, of the poem's relationships with other poems, by Eliot or by other poets, and no discussions of the poem's place in Eliot's career or in the literary or other context of the time or in the tradition. It differs in this from other guides and interpretations that have been published. In George Williamson's *Reader's Guide to T.S.Eliot: A Poem-by-Poem Analysis* (The Noonday Press, New York, 1957) the treatment of *Prufrock* stays remote from the narrative, selecting and 'associating' occasional details, with much general commentary and discussion of Eliot's methods and procedures; there is no indication of the poem's setting, characters or plot, structure or technique. Hugh Kenner, in *The Invisible Poet: T.S.Eliot* (Mc Dowell, Obolensky, New York, 1959), in a state of blankness before the poem as a whole, finds in *Prufrock* a world of words that have lost their connection with the active world, an accumulation of memorable effects whose workings he examines at length. John Berryman, writing on 'Prufrock's Dilemma' in *The Freedom of the Poet* (Farrar, Strauss and Giroux, New York, 1976), is clear about the plot and Prufrock's character, and deals closely with occasional detail; but he imposes structures from the spiritual history of man and the scientific revolutions of Darwin and Freud, and in astronomy; with speculations on questions of tone, quoting Laforgue, Elizabethan drama and Henry James, with illustrative matter from Kafka and others; all of these matters interfering with a primary appreciation of the poem – although illuminating once the poem has been absorbed on its own terms. Helen Vendler, in *Coming of Age as a Poet* (Harvard University Press, 2003), examines the poem as the first in which the young Eliot achieved his full poetic self, and makes comments on style and form; there are useful observations on the plot but a full reading is latent.

*

It is accepted that there are no absolute readings – especially in modern poetry, where the grounds for communication are often given sparingly; but also in the clearest-seeming verse, as with Shakespeare's sonnets – given the organic, and finally unlimited, possibilities in the detail of communication itself, where each reader's unique experience is brought to bear. But with adequate readings of a good poem the differences should be marginal, and not significant.

29

When in disgrace with Fortune and mens eyes,
I all alone beweepe my out-cast state,
And trouble deafe heaven with my bootlesse cries,
And looke upon my selfe and curse my fate,
Wishing me like to one more rich in hope,
Featur'd like him, like him with friends possest,
Desiring this mans art, and that mans skope,
With what I most enjoy contented least,
Yet in these thoughts my selfe almost despising,
Haplye I think on thee, and then my state,
(Like to the Larke at breake of daye arising)
From sullen earth sings hymns at Heavens gate,
For thy sweet love remembered such wealth brings,
That then I skorne to change my state with Kings.

30

When to the Sessions of sweet silent thought,
I summon up remembrance of things past,
I sigh the lacke of many a thing I sought,
And with old woes new waile my dear times waste:
Then can I drowne an eye unused to flow
For precious friends hid in deaths dateles night,
And weepe afresh love's long since canceld woe,
And mone th'expence of many a vannisht sight.
Then can I greeve at greevances fore-gon,
And heavily from woe to woe tell ore
The sad account of fore-bemoaned mone,
Which I new pay as if not payd before.
But if the while I thinke on thee (deare friend)
All losses are restored, and sorrowes end.

Shakespeare: *Sonnet 29*

First quatrain

Lines 1 and 2 — Noting that the syntax is suspended with the first word; and registering the opening scene :

A condition of isolation and shame, rejected by circumstance and by mankind. Regarded with ignominy in the eyes of men; his own eyes pouring tears.

Line 3 — The rejection equated with the expulsion from Eden. The private weeping now an outcry, complaining – and looking – toward Heaven; Heaven deaf; the cries unavailing.

Line 4 — The cries – and the regard of the eyes – turned back with curses upon the self.

A first quatrain of emotional and sensual extremes. Intense in imagery, so that the word 'disgrace' reads as the actual deprivation of grace, and the word 'outcast' as the act of casting out; the eye imagery strong in line 4 so that the outcast – disgraced in men's eyes in line 1 – is disgraced in his own eyes also.

Second quatrain

Lines 5 – 8 — The syntax still suspended. The basis given for the emotions of the first quatrain; the standards against which the complaints are measured : others more gifted by circumstance – one more gifted with looks, another with ease of friendship; one colleague with a particular technical skill, another with a range of theme, so that even in his chosen calling he is unsatisfied.

The second quatrain, without imagery, empties the sonnet of the extremes of the first.

Third quatrain

The extremes of the first quatrain, and their removal in the second, prepare for a third quatrain of dramatic effect.

Line 9

The solutions begin : of syntax (“Yet”); and of the emotional crisis (“almost”).

Line 10

The happy accident (“Haplye”) occurs on a memory of the beloved[*], initiating a change in the outcast state. This is the second use of ‘state’ in a rhyming position, readying it for a change of meaning.

Line 11

His state, rising like a lark – from nowhere, out of the dark into the light – with tiny explosive effect (a small richness of dentals and three small ‘k’s in a setting of open vowels). . .

Line 12

. . . gives voice to the outcast world. The voice is tiny, and Heaven’s gate remains shut, but the voice is singing

---

* The two previous sonnets having dealt with the pain of the beloved’s absence

hymns and no longer complaining. The imagery of the first quatrain restored, transfigured.

Lines 13 and 14 Ending with a couplet of lowered intensity : the problem solved; the argument proven. And a third use of 'state', the meaning enhanced by "Kings", and the introduction of the idea of wealth.

The concept of wealth is treated in the next sonnet.

Shakespeare: *Sonnet 30*

First quatrain

Lines 1 and 2	The image of a judicial assembly established, in an atmosphere of pleasant nostalgia. Memories called up from the past for silent scrutiny.
Line 3	Nostalgia turning to melancholy, quiet – but sighing, no longer silent, with the memory of things sought in the past, and not achieved.
Line 4	The memory sharpening, the sigh increasing to a wail, with the renewed painful awareness of things once possible and let pass, or achieved and squandered; key words 'waile' and 'waste'. The judicial assembly reduced, now, to the one.

Second quatrain

Line 5	With the solitary, sharpened memory – and accompanying the wail – tears that had flowed once for the loss, and ceased, flow again as though for the first time. . .
Line 6	. . .for the loss of precious friends lost in death's timeless dark;
Lines 7 & 8	weeping once again for the grief that had healed in a past love, and lamenting again the cost, or loss, of past experience.

Beginning with 'dear' and 'waste' in line 4; and developing through 'precious', 'dateles', 'canceld' and 'expence'; the idea of loving friendship has combined with that of accountancy and wealth. The woe for lost friendship is a debt due, and presented again for payment – dateless, that was thought cancelled. Key words are 'woe' and 'mone'.

Third quatrain

Lines 9-12 — The full account presented for payment. The uncancelled woes lamented and counted over heavily, as by an accountant or clerk, and paid again as if for the first time, with the repeated excessive open vowel sounds of 'woe' from line 7 and 'mone' from line 8.

Lines 13 & 14 — Tensions of sense and sound solved in a simple couplet. All losses, and sorrows, made good by the thought of the dear friend. After the excessively articulated mourning of lines 10 to 12 it is difficult to articulate line 13 without exercising the muscles of a smile.

The Tower

I

What shall I do with this absurdity –
O heart, O troubled heart – this caricature,
Decrepit age that has been tied to me
As to a dog's tail?
Never had I more
Excited, passionate, fantastical
Imagination, nor an ear and eye
That more expected the impossible –
No, not in boyhood when with rod and fly,
Or the humbler worm, I climbed Ben Bulben's back
And had the livelong summer day to spend.
It seems that I must bid the Muse go pack,
Choose Plato and Plotinus for a friend
Until imagination, ear and eye,
Can be content with argument and deal
In abstract things; or be derided by
A sort of battered kettle at the heel.

II

I pace upon the battlements and stare
On the foundations of a house, or where
Tree, like a sooty finger, starts from the earth;
And send imagination forth (1)
Under the day's declining beam, and call
Images and memories
From ruin or from ancient trees,
For I would ask a question of them all.

Beyond that ridge lived Mrs French, and once
When every silver candlestick or sconce
Lit up the dark mahogany and the wine,
A serving-man, that could divine (2)
That most respected lady's every wish,
Ran and with the garden shears

Clipped an insolent farmer's ears
And brought them in a little covered dish.

Some few remembered still when I was young
A peasant girl commended by a song,
Who'd lived somewhere upon that rocky place,
And praised the colour of her face, (3)
And had the greater joy in praising her,
Remembering that, if walked she there,
Farmers jostled at the fair
So great a glory did the song confer.

And certain men, being maddened by those rhymes,
Or else by toasting her a score of times,
Rose from the table and declared it right
To test their fancy by their sight; (4)
But they mistook the brightness of the moon
For the prosaic light of day –
Music had driven their wits astray –
And one was drowned in the great bog of Cloone.

Strange, but the man who made the song was blind;
Yet, now I have considered it, I find
That nothing strange; the tragedy began (5)
With Homer that was a blind man,
And Helen has all living hearts betrayed.
O may the moon and sunlight seem
One inextricable beam,
For if I triumph I must make men mad.

And I myself created Hanrahan
And drove him drunk or sober through the dawn
From somewhere in the neighbouring cottages.
Caught by an old man's juggleries (6)
He stumbled, tumbled, fumbled to and fro
And had but broken knees for hire
And horrible splendour of desire;
I thought it all out twenty years ago:

Good fellows shuffled cards in an old bawn;
And when that ancient ruffian's turn was on
He so bewitched the cards under his thumb
That all but the one card became (7)
A pack of hounds and not a pack of cards,
And that he changed into a hare.
Hanrahan rose in frenzy there
And followed up those baying creatures towards –

O towards I have forgotten what – enough!
I must recall a man that neither love
Nor music nor an enemy's clipped ear
Could, he was so harried, cheer; (8)
A figure that has grown so fabulous
There's not a neighbour left to say
When he finished his dog's day:
An ancient bankrupt master of this house.

Before that ruin came, for centuries,
Rough men-at-arms, cross-gartered to the knees
Or shod in iron, climbed the narrow stairs,
And certain men-at-arms there were (9)
Whose images, in the Great Memory stored,
Come with loud cry and panting breast
To break upon a sleeper's rest
While their great wooden dice beat on the board.

As I would question all, come all who can;
Come old, necessitous, half-mounted man;
And bring beauty's blind rambling celebrant;
The red man the juggler sent
Through God-forsaken meadows; Mrs French (10)
Gifted with so fine an ear;
The man drowned in a bog's mire,
When mocking Muses chose the country wench.

Did all old men and women, rich and poor,
Who trod upon these rocks or passed this door,
Whether in public or in secret rage
As I do now against old age? (11)
But I have found an answer in those eyes
That are impatient to be gone;
Go therefore; but leave Hanrahan,
For I need all his mighty memories.

Old lecher with a love on every wind,
Bring up out of that deep considering mind
All that you have discovered in the grave,
For it is certain that you have (12)
Reckoned up every unforeknown, unseeing
Plunge, lured by a softening eye,
Or by a touch or a sigh,
Into the labyrinth of another's being;

Does the imagination dwell the most
Upon a woman won or woman lost?
If on the lost, admit you turned aside (13)
From a great labyrinth out of pride,
Cowardice, some silly over-subtle thought
Or anything called conscience once;
And that if memory recur, the sun's
Under eclipse and the day blotted out.

III

It is time that I wrote my will;
I choose upstanding men
That climb the streams until
The fountain leap, and at dawn
Drop their cast at the side
Of dripping stone; I declare
They shall inherit my pride,
The pride of people that were
Bound neither to Cause nor to State,
Neither to slaves that were spat on,

Nor to the tyrants that spat,
The people of Burke and of Grattan
That gave, though free to refuse –
Pride, like that of the morn,
When the headlong light is loose,
Or that of the fabulous horn,
Or that of the sudden shower
When all streams are dry,
Or that of the hour
When the swan must fix his eye
Upon a fading gleam,
Float out upon a long
Last reach of glittering stream
And there sing his last song.
And I declare my faith:
I mock Plotinus' thought
And cry in Plato's teeth,
Death and life were not
Till man made up the whole,
Made lock, stock and barrel
Out of his bitter soul,
Aye, sun and moon and star, all,
And further add to that
That, being dead, we rise,
Dream and so create
Translunar Paradise.
I have prepared my peace
With learned Italian things
And the proud stones of Greece,
Poet's imaginings
And memories of love,
Memories of the words of women,
All those things whereof
Man makes a superhuman
Mirror-resembling dream.

As at the loophole there
The daws chatter and scream,
And drop twigs layer upon layer.

When they have mounted up,
The mother bird will rest
On their hollow top,
And so warm her wild nest.

I leave both faith and pride
To young upstanding men
Climbing the mountain-side,
That under bursting dawn
They may drop a fly;
Being of that metal made
Till it was broken by
This sedentary trade.

Now shall I make my soul,
Compelling it to study
In a learned school
Till the wreck of body,
Slow decay of blood,
Testy delirium
Or dull decrepitude,
Or what worse evil come –
The death of friends, or death
Of every brilliant eye
That made a catch in the breath –
Seem but the clouds of the sky
When the horizon fades;
Or a bird's sleepy cry
Among the deepening shades.

1926

W.B.Yeats : "The Tower"

"The Tower" is a poem in three parts, provoked by growing pressures of old age: part I a protest at the discrepancy between the poet's continuing imaginative liveliness and growing bodily limitations; part II a survey of the surrounding landscape from the battlements of the tower, and the summoning of a tribunal of local figures from legend and the past, to put two questions arising at the end of life; in part III the poet considers his will, and prepares for death.

Part I

Lines 1-4	A protest – rhetorical, half serious – at old age, as it is attached mischievously to the body, like something tied to a dog's tail,
Lines 5-8	while passion and excitement, imagination and the senses, are still at their most intense;
Lines 9-11	no less than in high youth – in lines establishing the height of passion and imaginative excitement, in the poet's case, in years of boyhood, climbing the hills and fishing in solitude.
Lines 12-17	The scheme of the opening lines made clear. The imagination and the senses, passion and excitement – as they deal in concrete things – are appropriate to youth, with the Muse as proper companion. Reason – dealing in abstract things – is appropriate to age, with philosophers for companions. The intensities of youth, lasting into age, are incongruous. Old age, unfit for the muse, and attached to the tail, is identified as a battered kettle.

Part II

First Stanza

Lines 18-20 The tower. A setting on the battlements, looking out past the ruins of a house and the black stump of a tree.

(For a speaker troubled by bodily decrepitude there seems a strong verbal excess in the opening line.)

Lines 21-25 It is the close of day, matching the end of life. In a personal ceremony, the poet summons in imagination certain spirits from the ruins of the house, and from among the trees of the neighbourhood, to put a question.

Second Stanza

Lines 26-33 The first spirit, summoned from over a nearby hill, is a member of the Ascendancy, remembered in an incident of excess, arising out of the tyrannous relationship between landlord and peasantry.

Third and Fourth Stanzas

The second spirit, remembered on another occasion of excess, is a man of the people – maddened by drink, the moon and a song.

Lines 34-36 The subject of the song: a peasant girl of the neighbourhood, remembered through the generations because of the song. . .

Lines 37-41 . . .and famous because of the song in her own time;

Lines 42-45 so famous that it was decided on a drunken occasion to check the song, by the light of the moon, against the reality,

Lines 46-49 — and the spirit now being summoned lost his life in the extreme attempt – so earning his place on the tribunal.

Fifth Stanza

Lines 50-52 — An apparent deviation from the ceremony, to consider the fact that the celebrant of such beauty – the poet Raftery – was blind;

Lines 52-54 — to find a precursor in blind Homer, who immortalised Helen*;

Lines 55-57 — to introduce the poet himself into the poem with these two poets, making men mad with poetry – the moon and sun fused in an excess; (and requiring, if the structure is to be complete, a woman to immortalise, and blindness of the poet's part). And to include – as will appear – Blind Raftery on the tribunal.

Sixth and Seventh Stanzas

Lines 58-65 — The poet summons a fourth spirit from "somewhere in the neighbouring cottages": Red Hanrahan, a character of extreme desire – a creation of his own.

Lines 66-73 — Hanrahan, rising from the card-table, pursuing the magical hunt across the country-side, and vanishing into the past. . .

Eighth Stanza

Lines 74-81 — . . .the setting returns to the battlement. A summary of the tribunal begins, and a final member is called up from inside the tower: a former occupant,

*It being a matter for the reader's consideration how far "Helen has all living hearts betrayed"

Ninth Stanza

Lines 82-89	in whose hands it fell into ruin, ending the generations of occupation, leaving it empty, in a last extreme – except as it is occupied by night, when the ghosts of the first Normans appear, to disturb the present generations.

Tenth Stanza

Lines 90-97	The tribunal summarised: the former owner of the tower; Blind Raftery; Red Hanrahan; Mrs. French, burdened with one of Yeats's rare jokes; the drunken man, who died to check the accuracy of a song. And "all who can" – who may include the Norman ghosts.

Eleventh Stanza

Lines 98-101	The question is put;
Lines 102/103	the question so shallow that the various spirits are impatient to be released.
Lines 104/105	Leaving only Hanrahan, the figure created by Yeats himself, for the real question,

Twelfth Stanza

Lines 106-113	for which he is especially qualified, by his wide and casual – and profound and particular – experience of love.

Thirteenth Stanza

Lines 114/115	The question is put with directness;
Lines 116-119	and the answer given, with brutality, in the question itself. So that even Hanrahan was unnecessary.

The poem speaks direct. The poet on the battlement admits, or claims, that he chose wrongly; that he has spent his life with the wrong woman; and that (as the fifth stanza

Lines 120-121 requires) the sun darkens when he remembers the woman lost, and he is blinded with emotion.

Part III

Lines 122-127 He considers his will. It is an enclosed gesture: for his heirs he chooses essentially himself when young, fishing in the mountain streams; climbing in the dawn 'until/ The fountain leap' – emphasising imagery of source and new beginning.

Lines 127-134 For his legacy, his pride – the pride of a morally and intellectually liberal and uncommitted middle class, belonging neither to tyrannous Ascendancy nor to ignominious peasantry;

Lines 135-139 a pride associated, again, with the imaginative excitement of boyhood, with imagery of dawnlight and fountain, horn of plenty and refreshment at the source;

Lines 140-145 a pride also of evening and peace, a swan song of fulfilment at the end of life.

Lines 146-149 He declares and considers his faith, dismissing the philosophers ordinarily appropriate to old age, and the abstract considerations of death and life. There is no trace of religious faith

Lines 150-153 – Mankind, bitter in nature and experience, is all there is, on earth or elsewhere.

Lines 154-157 If there is an afterlife, it is based on nothing but mankind.

Lines 158-163 He summarises the valuable findings of a life, the material out of which he has contrived an understanding: things from the Mediterranean past, ancient and Renaissance; poetry; the love and the words of women;

Lines 164-166 matter with which a man can make a dream-construct – its parts reflecting among themselves, so that it seems more than it is.

Lines 167-169 An image of that construct close at hand: a bird's nest on the battlement, put together from bits and pieces, layer upon layer,

Lines 170-173 by daws chattering and screaming – an image of the human species; the present generation warm on the hollow top.

Lines 174-176 With the cosmic limits established, and meaning restricted to mankind, he leaves his legacy of faith and pride to those only in the next generation who will repeat his own beginnings. It is a closed gesture – but an image of possible rebirth.

Lines 177/178 And his wish is that his chosen heirs – with his legacy of pride and faith – will 'drop a fly'.

It is a gesture of great risk, risking bathos. With the reader required to decide whether it is successful; saved by the confident diction, and the power of the episode and the imagery that has placed greatest imaginative intensity in boyhood, fishing in solitude in the dawn. And – if the decision is positive – with the reader free to speculate profoundly on the image of dropping a lure into a stream, and a source on a mountain-top.

Lines 179-181 Aware of his active and imaginative youth, and his sedentary and imaginative present . . .

Lines 182-end . . . he turns away from the pointless ceremony.

He will tackle his bitter soul, continuing his old man's studies, until even old age is at an end, with the death of friends, the death of the 'woman lost' (lines 191/2), his own death – matching the end of the day, declining now into the dark – and the ending of his generation : the daws fallen silent.

Note As to the rhyming of 'Grattan' / 'spat on', 'barrel' / 'star, all' : the reader needs to decide on the success of this; whether the ongoing strength of the poem is sufficient at each point not to be interrupted by the technical extremity of the gesture.

T.S.Eliot: *The Love Song of J. Alfred Prufrock*

Title A deviation, awkward or comic, from the standard love song. The name ‘Prufrock’ – with elements of ‘prudery’, ‘prudence’ and ‘frock’ – suggests a cautious, formal lover; not masculine. The tone established by the whole title would work against any masculine suggestion, such as ‘proof’ and ‘rock’.

Epigraph The quotation from Dante’s *Inferno* emphasises the deviation, with the setting in Hell. The voice of the suffering spirit establishes the scene of the poem’s beginning at the margin of the ordinary world:

> If I thought that I was going to reply
> To one who might return once more to the world
> This flame of fire would never flicker again.
>
> But since there never was return to that world
> By one alive, if I have heard it truly,
> I can reply without any fear of shame.

A reference to the Divine Comedy prepares for a dual persona, guide and companion. And a love song with a reference to Dante might suggest a love remote and inaccessible, as for Beatrice.

*

Lines 1-3 Prufrock sets out at evening with an unidentified companion. There is a low bank of cloud, outlined to Prufrock’s imagination like a patient lying flat under a sheet on an operating table. Any traditional poetic expectations, from the idea of love song and from the rhythms and content of the first two lines – and that might have survived the title and epigraph – are dismissed by this inert and unhealthy image, expressed with accuracy and economy in a language remote from established poetic diction.

Lines 4-7 The setting is a poor area in a modern city; described in terms conveying the coarseness, poverty and unease of the inhabitants. The 'muttering' is of people, but could include the muttering of gas lamps in streets and houses. Images are of cheap business, transience and spitting; observed with detachment, but familiarity.

The infernal setting is a slum at night, the narrator prowling.

Lines 8-12 The streets are allegorical, leading toward somewhere meaningful. Their layout is repetitive and insistent, adding to the unease. The narrator is implicated in the allegory, being urged toward a particular end. It is increasingly probable, from the privacy of detail and sensual intimacy of the narrative, that he is alone – the 'you' in line 10 and the 'us' in line 12 are the narrator and companion in a dual awareness.

The words 'tedious', 'insidious' and 'overwhelming' emerge from the surrounding coarseness, enacting the narrator's fastidiousness. They enact also a hesitation, but this hesitation is dismissed in a brisk double rhyme.

Prufrock, alone and ruminating, prowling the mean streets, is on his way toward a crucial destination. He is hesitant and not confident, but urges himself on his way with a quick gesture.

Lines 13-14 A mental image of his destination. An elegant and remote world: 'Beatrice' and her companions, at their paradisal routines of beauty and art.

Lines 15-19 A new poetic procedure. The narrative intensifies from the allegorical to the imagistic. Prufrock indulges in an imaginative exercise, visualising the surrounding smoke and fog as an animal sensually investigating its surroundings and its own nature – as he is doing. The animal is presented intimately; the contact is not pleasant, but not unfriendly. The nature of the setting is confirmed, in the fog and smoke and wet corners, pools and drains and sooty chimneys.

Lines 20-22 Details of the animal accumulate, and particularise. It is a cat, nervously seeking and finding peace, on a terrace, at a particular house. Finding peace there, it is freed of its inward preoccupation with squalid detail; notes the serenity of the surrounding dark; and falls asleep.

The cat is Prufrock's image of his own state of mind. The terrace and the house are images of his destination. He finds peace in an imagined intimacy there. Serenity is conveyed in a full and easy rhyme.

Lines 23-27 Prufrock is uneasy again. His unease, as well as his imagined peace, is associated with his destination. He is preparing himself for a difficult encounter. The difficulty is enacted by the repetition in line 26 of the phrase 'there will be time', associated with his indecision; by the mirrored nouns and verb in line 27; and by the need 'To prepare'.

Lines 28-36 It will be a polite social encounter, with toast and tea and casual questions. But the scale of the encounter, as it approaches, grows in Prufrock's mind. He finds a traditional – a historic – dimension in his predicament : with the Biblical 'murder and create', and with the title of Hesiod's classic of social behaviour, in 'works and days of hands'. And some of the experience as he foresees it is not social in the ordinary way : hands that 'lift and drop a question on your plate' are more threatening than polite. They leave Prufrock with a flutter of indecisiveness – enacted in the repetitions of lines 32 and 33. And with a clear image – repeated – of his destination : formal and forbidding.

Lines 37-46 The final moment before the encounter, imagined. The last moment for indecision : Prufrock ascending the stairs alone. Indecisiveness is given free play, with its repeated phrases, including the associated phrase 'there will be time', and its variations, from earlier in the poem. To put the question, offering his love song, would be to risk rejection, upsetting his world and his place in it. He sees himself as the beloved and her companions would see him. And as he is : dressed especially for the occasion, past his prime, determined and not quite adequate. There is a narrow emphasis in the rhyming of 'thin' (twice), 'chin' and 'pin'. He sees himself descending the stairs, the encounter shirked at the last moment, or the question put and rejected; and imagines the womanly comments at his failure of will or the rejection. There is no place in his imagination for either outcome – certainly not for the offering of a love song. He does not presume. He does not 'dare / Disturb the universe'.

Lines 47-8 The final minute of indecision; enacted, busy with decisions and revisions; ending – charged with negatives – on ‘reverse’.

Lines 49-67 Prufrock considers the grounds for his negative decision, in three sections, each consideration ending with the same rhetorical question :

Considering the social requirements; he is familiar with these and can record them accurately, and himself as he plays his part, but he is detached and does not belong. (Lines 49-54)

Considering the reason for his detachment; in the kinds of conversation that proceed at conventional level, for the purpose of social assessment, there is an ill-fitting primal element in his nature which he must conceal. (Lines 55-61)

Considering the sensual demands of the imagined proposal, Prufrock’s attention, and will, are straying among the details of her body and perfume and dress; the individuality of the beloved blurring among the plurality of women. (Lines 62-67)

Lines 68-9 The rhetorical question (...how should I presume...) put after each of these considerations – as to the possibility of a proposal to the beloved (and with a negative answer) – is put once more. With the additional question: how a proposal might have begun.

Lines 70-80 Prufrock considers two ways in which he might have presumed to begin a proposal.

By presenting himself in his inner aspect, in the context of mean realities recorded in the opening section of the poem. This possibility, offensive and unfitting, is dismissed at once, with an image of his unfit nature : predatory and silent – designed essentially for a different element. He recognises this with exasperation. (Lines 70-74)

Or by offering himself in his polite, outer aspect, as embodied earlier in the shape of a cat: stretched peacefully on the floor between himself and the beloved, smoothed by her fingers. But in his polite aspect he lacks the will to act. (Lines 75-80)

The separate components of his nature conflict.

Lines 81-86 The effect is that, even in failure, he lacks stature. No matter how painfully he might prepare for a leading role : as martyred prophet, with severed head offered to Salome on a platter (an extreme image of the possible proposal) there would be something incongruous to spoil the effect. Conventional society, to its meanest attendant, would dismiss his presumption with amusement. The incongruity is emphasised in the double rhyming of 'fingers. . . malingers', 'ices. . . crises', 'platter. . . matter', 'flicker. . . snicker'.

His decision against the attempt is complete.

Lines 87-98 Prufrock resumes his solitary prowl. The decision made, the ordeal refused, there is an ease in the tone and in the open rhyming.

He analyses his decision. Whether it would have been worth it : to have gathered all his social confidence and put the question. To have chosen the moment, loaded for him with such significance; to have offered his entire being, and met only with a frigid dismissal – the offer, intensely expressed, amounting merely to a faux pas. It would not have been worth it.

The ease following his decision is enacted in a stable rhythm, mainly iambic pentameter; the rhymes open, simple and monosyllabic. Only the unrhymed 'question' stands out.

Lines 99-110 The relief is short. Refusal makes for a negative, not a positive, ease. Prufrock remains inadequate. The rhythms of uneasiness return, with Prufrock thinking still of the failed proposal : it was the reason he set out. He is dogged still by the ignominious image of a probable rejection. The particulars of the setting, of the destination, and of his possible attempt, trail away into speechlessness in line 104. In line 105 his nervous interior, the inarticulate site of his unease, dominates in an image of artificial vivid reality, echoing the poem's unhealthy opening images.

*

Lines 111-119 It is over. Prufrock, having set out hesitantly to play a principal part, confirms that he is comfortable only in a minor role, cautious and meticulous; almost ridiculous. Not Hamlet, but Polonius. 'Almost, at times, the Fool'. Offering a love song, he would have mistaken his part.

Lines 120-end A full image of the life that awaits Prufrock : marginal and uninvolved, the risk not taken. He is at the edge of the ocean, and of life, paddling in the water with white flannel trousers rolled up. The things on his mind are trivial, even in the world of convention : his uncertain digestion; whether he might arrange his hair to cover the (unmartyred) bald spot. He is still allegorically at the edge of things, functioning neither in the ocean (where he has imagined himself earlier, predatory in the depths) nor in the world of men.

Images of women and polite convention, at one extreme of the poem, have presented an inaccessible world. Images of a brutal submarine reality, at the other extreme, have presented another world, also inaccessible. At the close of the poem the two worlds converge : mermaids singing on the ocean, woman-figures alluring the hero to their other world.

They are not singing to Prufrock. He is not a hero. He only overhears them. But there is the consolation that he does not suffer the heroic fate. He can enter the forbidden world at one remove; he can overhear the song of the sirens and survive. His place is at the edge. He is at home imaginatively in the world of the sirens, and in worlds other than theirs. In the world of images he is a chronicler, handling detail with sensual and psychological accuracy, uninvolved and at ease.

There are significant positive signs. The poem at the close divides into a strict and easeful variant of the terza rima, as in the Divine Comedy. And for the last three lines the dual narrator returns, in a second imagined encounter, as Prufrock follows the mermaids out to sea, in lines of expertise and power, finally in his proper element, chosen and wreathed with garlands, filling a major role in the company of lovely women, for as long as the reality remains an imagined one, with no intrusion from the actual world.

Note There are two non-textual matters of possible relevance in a reading of the poem.

T.S.Eliot has been reported as denying that the 'you' is an alter ego; as saying that there is a narrator and 'an unidentified male companion'. It is possible to read the poem in this way (with the companion playing no part), as far as line 14. But from line 15 the narrative is private and internal, with no trace of a companion, even as alter ego (apart from a verbal echo in line 31) until line 129.

Early unpublished manuscript poems of Eliot collected in *Inventions of the March Hare*, ed. Christopher Ricks (Harcourt Brace; San Diego, New York, London, 1996), include an early version of *The Love Song of J. Alfred Prufrock*. This is virtually identical with the final version; with a subtitle 'Prufrock Among the Women'; a different epigraph: two lines from the *Purgatorio*, Canto XXVI, in which the spirit of Arnaut Daniel asks to be remembered and returns to the cleansing fire; and 36 additional lines of verse. These consist of 32 lines after line 72 of the final version and 4 lines after line 74, apparently in a different hand and together given the title 'Prufrock's Pervigilium'. They contain additional detail of squalid night-time description and feline imagery, with explicit reference to the narrator's 'fever' and 'Madness', singing and chattering. Their inclusion would reveal more of the nervous Prufrock, with ill-fitting predatory parts, over-watchful at social events. Their elimination leaves his complex outline clearer.

pepper

canister

Readings in Poetry is number 25 in the Peppercanister series by Thomas Kinsella. It is set in 11 point Times New Roman and published in a paperback edition of 500 copies.

First published February 2006